ANIMALS OF THE OCEANS

S0-BUC-747

PENGUINS

JUDITH HODGE

BARRON'S

CONTENTS

INTRODUCTION

Penguins are members of a family of flightless sea birds found only in the Southern Hemisphere. Most people imagine penguins against a backdrop of ice and snow. In fact, they live in many different environments, ranging from tall grass to rocky shores to hot areas near the equator. Some even nest in trees on the Snares Islands off the coast of New Zealand.

Their real home, though, is the ocean and penguins spend most of their lives in the water. They only come ashore to lay their eggs and raise their young.

On land penguins walk with a clumsy waddle, the result of having feet directly under their bodies. But penguins are excellent swimmers and they glide gracefully through the water.

Their ancestors could probably fly. Penguins are thought to be related to today's diving petrels and auks. These are Northern Hemisphere birds that fly poorly but swim well using their wings. Over millions of years penguins lost the power of flight and their wings became flippers.

Penguins have adapted both to life underwater and to the cold temperatures of the Antarctic habitat. Like all birds, they are warm-blooded. They have two layers of short, thick feathers that act as a waterproof coat and trap

body heat. In the species that live farthest south, even the flippers are covered in scale-like feathers. Penguins also have a thick layer of fat, or blubber, to keep them warm.

Above: The only flying the modern-day penguin does is underwater. They propel themselves through water with the flying movements of their flippers. The legs are used like rudders, for steering.

Penguins have never lived north of the equator. This is because they are so well-insulated that tropical waters are too warm for them.

DIFFERENT KINDS OF PENGUINS

There is some debate as to how many species of penguins there are—numbers vary from 16 to 18. This is because some scientists count certain types of penguin as subspecies rather than as species in their own right.

All kinds of penguins have a similar body shape and form. But from the chest up, each species has distinctive feather markings, or colored plumes and skin patterns. Members of the crested family, for example, have long yellow or orange feathers above their eyes that look like eyebrows.

Penguins vary greatly in size. The emperor is the tallest at about 4 feet, 3 inches, almost three times the height of the smallest, the little blue. In earlier times penguins looked very different from each other and were much larger than present-day species. Fossil bones have been found of a species that was nearly 5 feet tall.

Fossils found in New Zealand also show that penguins lived there more than 55 to 60 million

The emperor penguin (top) and the little blue penguin (left) vary greatly in both size and lifestyle.

Most species of penguin nest in colonies called rookeries, which can hold as many as a million birds.

years ago. It was probably around the coasts of New Zealand that the birds first developed.

Penguins now live on the shores of the continents and islands throughout the Southern Hemisphere, from the southern coasts of South America, South Africa, Australia, New Zealand and its subantarctic islands, as well as Antarctica. In fact, wherever there are islands, you'll find penguins living on them.

EMPEROR PENGUINS

Emperor penguins have amazing lives. They are masters of the icy Antarctic, living farther south than any other penguin and breeding in the harshest climate of any species on earth.

With striking patches of orange-yellow under its head and standing more than 4 feet tall, the emperor lives up to its name. It is not only the biggest penguin but the deepest diver, hunting fish and squid in the ocean at depths of up to nearly a quarter of a mile.

Emperor and king penguins belong to the same family and share some features, although they live in different habitats. There are about 40 colonies of emperor penguins around the antarctic continent. To cope with the cold, the species has developed a thick layer of fat and its feathers cover its feet and bill.

These penguins do not make nests. The female lays an egg that the male puts on his feet and covers with a thick fold of skin to keep it warm. The emperor males then huddle

"Porpoising" onto the sea ice is the easiest way for a heavy emperor penguin to get out of the water.

Right: The emperor often stands still for long lengths of time so that it uses less energy.

together incubating the eggs for two to three months during the bitter polar winter.

The females return with food when the chicks are newly hatched. If the chick hatches before the mother is back, the male feeds it a special substance called penguin's milk from his bill.

By spring the chicks are very large and almost ready to fledge (lose their down and grow real feathers). They are now able to fend for themselves at the only time of year when the sea ice is open and there is plenty of food.

Young chicks keep warm under the same fold of skin that protected the egg from the polar winter.

KING PENGUINS

At just over 3 feet in height, king penguins are nearly as tall as emperors but weigh about half as much. They have less fat because they live farther north in a slightly warmer climate.

Kings are a subantarctic species, breeding on islands in and around the antarctic region, such as South Georgia Island. They share this habitat with the family of crested penguins. King penguins are one of the most attractive penguin species. With their black heads, silvery-gray backs, yellow chests, and bright yellowy-orange patches shaped like commas on their cheeks, they are definitely the most photogenic!

The king penguins breed on raised beaches, muddy flats, and tussock meadows with easy access to the sea. Like the emperor, they look after the single egg on their feet, but in this species both the male and female share the task.

Their colonies are busy, noisy places with separate areas for breeding, molting, and roosting birds. Chicks are born

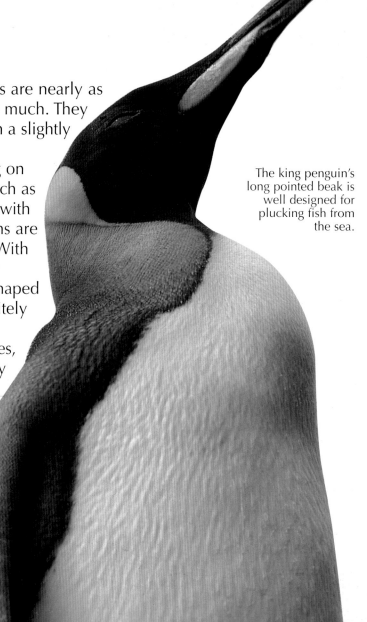

The king penguin's long pointed beak is well designed for plucking fish from the sea.

Emperor and king penguins stand with their eggs on their feet. The eggs themselves are large with thick shells, strong enough to do without the protection of a nest.

with a fluffy layer of down. There is an overlap of generations because it takes 15 months to raise a chick and most kings breed every other year.

King penguins were hunted in large numbers for their oil in the 19th and 20th centuries, probably because they lived in such accessible places. The population has now recovered to more than a million pairs.

King penguin chicks are covered in brown fluffy down. Early explorers thought the chicks were a separate species because they looked so different from their parents.

BRUSH-TAILED PENGUINS: ADELIES

The antarctic continent and the islands in the southern oceans are also home to the brush-tailed penguins. These include the Adelie, chinstrap, and gentoo. All have long tailfeathers that stick out like a brush, which they use to sweep melted ice away from the nest.

Adelie penguins were first seen by the French explorer, Dumont d'Urville, when he led an expedition to Antarctica in 1839. The species lives the farthest south of the brush-tailed family, sharing the same extreme conditions as the emperor penguin.

They are even more heavily feathered than emperors. Adelies have feathers covering most of their faces, apart from a very small area of the bill. They are easy to recognize, with white rings around their eyes that stand out against their black heads.

Adelies are some of the most sociable penguins. They are usually seen in groups and

Adelies lay two eggs and raise (usually) two chicks.

breed in huge rookeries. There is an estimated 2.5 million pairs around Antarctica. Often the nesting places are as far as 50 miles from the edge of the sea ice, and the penguins have to walk for one or two days to reach them. To travel faster, Adelies will toboggan on their stomachs over the ice, using their feet and flippers to push themselves along.

The species is a medium-sized penguin with an average height of 28 inches. Despite their size, Adelies are not timid and will defend their territory fiercely from other penguins or people.

The penguins feed mostly on krill up to 30 miles offshore and at depths of up to 80 yards. They can often be seen near the edge of the ice, checking the water for leopard seals before taking the plunge.

CHINSTRAP and GENTOO PENGUINS

Chinstraps look like Adelies except for a thick black line, or chinstrap, across their throats. They are also slightly smaller and more aggressive, with screeching voices. Chinstraps will charge intruders who stray into their rookeries.

Both chinstraps and Adelies live in noisy penguin cities, often nesting next to each other. There are thought to be more chinstraps than any other penguin, with an estimated population of 12 to 13 million. They live mainly in the subantarctic but there are also large colonies on the antarctic peninsula.

Chinstraps often choose high nesting sites so that the snow melts around their nests first. This gives them the maximum time to raise their chicks. Chinstrap chicks hatch later than Adelie and gentoos but their growth rate is faster.

Gentoos are slightly larger than Adelies and chinstraps, but less aggressive. They have

The long, stiff tail feathers of chinstrap penguins help support them when they are resting.

Sea lions prey on gentoos and patrol the waters near colonies. For this reason the penguins often make their rookeries some distance inland.

Gentoos, along with chinstraps, Adelies and macaronis, make nests from stones, as there is no grass or material to make a softer nest in the Antarctic. Stone nests drain well when the ice melts.

orange beaks and a white marking above their eyes. *Gentoo* is a name for Hindus who wear white cotton caps, rather like the penguin's cap of white feathers across the top of its head.

The species lives the farthest north of all the brush-tailed penguins. Their range is from the extreme climate of the Antarctic Islands to more temperate places like the Falklands. Gentoos like to stay close to home and they can be found all year round in the Falklands. They breed on grassy, gently sloping ground near the sea, in smaller groupings than Adelies, with nests spread well apart. Like most penguins, though, they like to be in each other's company.

CRESTED PENGUINS: ROCKHOPPER and MACARONI

There are six species of crested penguins. They are found in the icy waters of the far south as well as on tussock-covered islands in much warmer climates. In spite of the wide difference of habitats, crested penguins, with their wild tufted eyebrows of yellowish feathers, are all very much alike.

Rockhoppers are the smallest species in the family. They have red eyes and a spiky crest of black feathers on top of their heads, as well as the trademark eyebrows. All crested penguins live in colonies and are aggressive, but the rockhoppers are especially so. They are only about 12 inches high, yet will attack anyone they think is a threat.

A surging sea and a long drop are no problem for the rockhopper penguin.

The birds live up to their name. They do a lot of jumping off low boulders and hop up steep, rocky slopes with both feet together. The penguins are so well padded that they seldom hurt themselves.

Macaronis are the largest and heaviest of the family and live the farthest south. They are named after the London Macaroni Club, a group of young male fashion setters in the late 1700s who wore very high wigs with tiny hats perched on top of them. The penguins have a bright yellowy-orange drooping crest and both their face and neck are dark.

Among the most numerous of penguins, there are an estimated 11 million breeding pairs of macaronis.

For both macaronis and rockhoppers, it is the male who looks after the chick while the female makes frequent journeys to the sea for food. This is usually a job shared by both sexes in penguin species.

Like all crested penguins, the rockhopper's crest lies flat against its head in the water but springs up again as the bird starts to dry off.

15

MORE CRESTED PENGUINS

The other four species of crested penguins live in very specific locations, in the seas south of New Zealand and Australia. Their nesting places are less bleak than the Antarctic, with a landscape of grass and trees.

The Snares crested penguin breeds only on the shores of Snares Islands, which lies south of New Zealand. These penguins are great nest-builders, making large nests of sticks and twigs lined with leaves. They have even been found nesting in the low branches of trees.

The Fiordland crested penguin is very shy and nests

Erect-crested penguins have a yellow crest and brown eyes.

in caves or among tree roots. It breeds in the forests of the Fiordland coast of New Zealand's South Island or on nearby islands. Snares crested and Fiordland crested penguins are very similar, though the Snares penguin has a white outline around its orange beak.

Erect-crested penguins are very noisy, sociable birds found in huge colonies on the subantarctic Antipodes and Bounty Islands. Nest sites can either be soft tussock grass or bare rock. The species is the only one that can raise or lower its crest, which is more stubby than the long feathers of the others.

Some scientists do not think of the royal crested as a separate species, but a subspecies of the macaroni. The main differences in appearance are the slightly larger size of the royals and the white feathers on their face and throats. They breed only on Macquarie Island, south of New Zealand, and are rarely found elsewhere.

Fiordland crested penguins nest in the hollows at the base of trees or in small caves, and line their nests with fern fronds and leaves.

RINGED PENGUINS

Ringed or banded penguins have bands of black on white throats and pink patches on their faces. Three species live around the South American coastline and another in South Africa. Ringed penguins have fewer feathers and less fat than their more southerly cousins. This is because they live in a warmer climate.

At 25 inches high, Magellanic penguins are the largest in this family, and they breed on the coast of southern South America and the Falkland Islands. The penguins were named for Ferdinand Magellan, the Spanish explorer on whose route they were first spotted by Europeans. Magellanics have a double black band

The African penguin has mottled feet, which are black and flesh-colored. They are also known as black-footed penguins.

Living so far north, the Galapagos penguin has bare patches of skin to help it lose heat.

across their chests; the other ringed species have a single band.

Humboldt or Peruvian penguins breed in small colonies along the west coasts of Chile and Peru and on nearby islands. The penguins feed in the cold, nutrient-rich waters of the Humboldt current, which supports the local anchovy fishery. The competition for food has led to a decline in their population.

The African penguin is also known as the cape, black-footed, spectacled, and jackass. It is the only species that breeds on the mainland and islands off the southern coasts of South Africa and the first penguin seen by Europeans. Its numbers are also dropping due to overfishing.

The Galapagos is the world's warmest-weather penguin. It lives on the Galapagos Islands near the equator and nests in shady places to keep out of the sun. The penguin is one of the rarest species, with only about 2,000 to 6,000 birds left.

Like the African or jackass penguin, Magellanics are well known for their loud, braying call.

LITTLE BLUE and YELLOW-EYED PENGUINS

The smallest penguin species is the little blue, also known as the fairy penguin. It is only 16 inches high and weighs about 3 pounds, with brilliant blue feathers.

Little blue penguins breed mainly in southern Australia and New Zealand, where five or six subspecies are recognized. One of these, the white-flippered, is sometimes called a separate species in its own right. It has a white band along the front of its flippers.

The little blue is the only nocturnal penguin and is very timid. It comes onto land late at night and returns to the sea at daylight. The only birds found ashore during the day are those courting, molting or sitting on nests.

Little blue penguins live in burrows in small colonies on the coasts and islands of New Zealand and southern Australia.

Little blue penguins burrow out well-hidden nests in sand dunes or under rocks.

One of the most unusual species is the yellow-eyed penguin, known as the *hoiho* (meaning noise-shouter in Maori). It lives in

Hoiho (above and left) are so shy that they usually will not come ashore if people are about.

the forests of New Zealand's South Island and on a few offshore islands. The penguin has pale cat-like eyes and light yellow feathers from the eyes to the back of the head.

Hoiho are the only penguins that do not live in any type of colony. The birds usually nest quietly among tussock grass close to the sea and stay near their breeding areas all year round. The species has been badly affected by the destruction of its habitat. Like the little blue penguin, it is preyed on by ferrets, stoats, and cats that eat its eggs and young. The hoiho is possibly the world's most endangered penguin.

THE PENGUIN'S BODY

Penguins are strange-looking birds. They have bottle-shaped bodies with a pointed front end and large webbed feet that tuck under the body. This is the perfect streamlined shape for moving quickly through water. Penguins swim at 4 to 6 mph, but can go twice as fast in short bursts.

Their wings have developed into hard, paddle-like flippers, better suited to pushing against water than air. Flying birds have light, hollow bones but a penguin's are solid and heavy. Penguins are built for diving, with well-muscled and insulated bodies, strong enough to swim in very rough seas.

As graceful as dolphins in water, the penguin's body shape means that it walks with a comical waddle ashore. Unlike other birds, penguins stand upright with straight backs. They

With such a thick layer of fat, or blubber, penguins are so well-adapted to the cold they sometimes have problems with overheating. To shed heat, penguins hold their flippers out, away from their body.

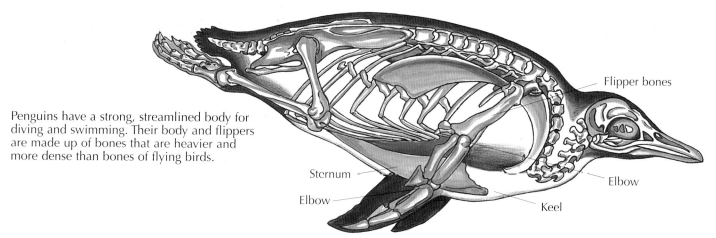

Penguins have a strong, streamlined body for diving and swimming. Their body and flippers are made up of bones that are heavier and more dense than bones of flying birds.

Flipper bones

Sternum

Elbow

Elbow

Keel

have short, stocky legs but can move quite quickly. Each foot has three hooked toes, which are used for grasping onto slippery rocks and ice. Strong bills act as an extra tool to help them up steep slopes.

A penguin's feathers are shorter than those of other birds. They are so tightly packed together that they look like seal fur. The birds spend a lot of time preening their feathers to keep them waterproof. Every year they grow a new coat to replace those that are worn and damaged. They must stay on land during the molt, as without a waterproof layer they would die of cold in the water.

Penguins "porpoise" to breathe when swimming fast underwater.

SENSES and COMMUNICATION

Penguins have good eyesight. They can change the shape of the lenses in their eyes so they can see well both on land and in water. In dark or murky seas, a penguin's large eyes can adapt to the low levels of light.

The birds use sound, not sight, to find their young. There could be up to 2,000 to 3,000 chicks in a crowded colony and parent and chick call continuously to home in on each other. Penguins within a species look so alike that they might walk past each other without recognition, but each bird has its individual call.

Penguin colonies are very noisy places as the birds use calls to communicate anger or attraction, or just to announce their presence. With so many birds nesting side by side, fights often break out with lots of squawking and slapping with flippers.

Different species make different noises. Kings have a trumpet sound while emperors trill a series of notes. Less musical is the scratchy

Meeting up with a partner always means a screech of welcome.

cooing of the Adelie and the braying of the African penguins, also known as jackasses.

Courtship among penguins involves special dances with dips, bows, curtsies, and calls. Each species has its own style, though the Adelies have the most elaborate behavior and the little blue the least. One of the most dramatic behaviors is the ecstatic display, performed by a number of species. This is when an unattached male pumps his chest several times, arches his head backwards, splays out his flippers, and gives a loud bray.

Penguin courtship often involves elaborate and colorful displays.

FEEDING and PREDATORS

Above: Chicks will often chase after a parent demanding food. Keeping their offspring well fed is a full-time job for all adult penguins.

All penguins eat some kind of fish or other marine creatures, though diets vary from species to species. The little blue and yellow-eyed penguins feed mostly on fish. Larger penguins, like the chinstraps, Adelies, and gentoos of the Antarctic, eat mainly shrimp-like krill. Kings and emperors are excellent divers and hunt deep-living prey such as squid.

Penguins don't filter-feed or strain out their food—they gulp up fish along with mouthfuls of water. The birds have special glands at the base of their bills to excrete excess salt from all the sea water they swallow. Bills are strong for gripping. Tongues and mouths are lined with backward-pointing, gristly spines for more help in grasping and swallowing wriggling prey.

One of the penguin's greatest enemies is the leopard seal. These ferocious animals pose little or no threat on land, but will patrol the shores waiting for penguins to enter the water. Other predators include fur seals and sea lions, as

Skuas sweep in on penguin colonies to snatch eggs and chicks from parents taken by surprise.

well as sharks in warmer seas and killer whales in the far south.

Skuas are birds that look like gulls. They will prey on vulnerable chicks and eggs at the edge of penguin colonies. Sometimes skuas work in pairs to separate a young penguin from its mother or other birds. Penguins in more temperate climates also face danger from introduced predators such as wild cats, ferrets, and stoats. The situation is critical for species like the little blue and yellow-eyed penguin.

Penguins feed their young on half-digested food that they store in their crop–an elastic-walled sac in their throat. The chick's beak fits right inside the adult's.

27

LIFE CYCLE

Most penguins breed in huge colonies, some with up to a million pairs. Only the yellow-eyed penguin has nests that are completely separate from each other, though other species live in smaller groups.

Penguins return to the same breeding places every year, even to the same nesting spot within the colony. Male and female pair bonds are often long-standing. Some species, like gentoo, stay together throughout the year. Others are reunited with their mates when they meet up at the same breeding area near the end of winter.

Nests are built with sticks, stones, grass, or whatever the birds can find. Most species lay either one or two eggs, but some lay up to four. The eggs have to be incubated for several weeks to give the unborn chicks time to develop.

Mating pairs share all the tasks, from nest-building to incubating eggs and feeding their offspring. Newborn chicks are kept warm by

Until they have completed molting and grown their adult feathers, chicks are dependent upon their parents.

In a creche young chicks are looked after by a few adults while parents are away. This means they are safe from attack by skuas and sheathbills.

Below: Penguins often return to the same nesting site each year, and mates share the job of raising chicks.

the parents until they are old enough to huddle together in a creche with other young penguins for warmth and protection. The parents still feed them at this stage. They only begin to fend for themselves when they are fully fledged (have grown adult feathers) and can enter the water.

At the end of the breeding season, adult penguins grow a new coat of feathers. Once this is done they can go back to their life at sea and the cycle begins all over again.

PENGUINS and PEOPLE

Penguins were a plentiful source of food and clothing for indigenous people in the Southern Hemisphere, such as the Maori in New Zealand. The Maori made the bird's feathered skins into cloaks and ate their eggs as well. But none of this had much effect on penguin numbers and there were still huge colonies when Europeans first saw them.

To early explorers, eating the meat of penguins made a welcome change from salted beef. Penguins that were not taken as scientific specimens ended up in the cooking pot. For many years people thought of penguins as fish with feathers, rather than birds that swam.

The slaughter of penguins for their oil devastated many colonies, particularly on subantarctic islands. The birds were preyed on following the decline of whale and seal populations. Killing penguins is now banned in countries like Australia and New Zealand, and some islands have become sanctuaries.

There is little known about the life of penguins at sea because transmitters are too big for tagging them. But censuses and studies on shore have still taught us a lot about their behavior.

Today, however, many species are still under threat. One of the greatest dangers comes from the destruction of penguin habitats by people. The African penguin is particularly at risk from

Penguins face danger at sea from marine rubbishlike plastic and fishing nets and oil spillage from tankers.

their numbers. The yellow-eyed and Galapagos penguins are also on the endangered list.

Of all the species, only the Antarctic penguins are flourishing. This is largely a result of more krill being available after hunters killed large numbers of baleen whales in the 19th and early 20th centuries. Even this trend may be short-lived as people are beginning to look at the rich fisheries of Antarctica.

oil spillages from tankers traveling close to its colonies. The mining of guano (dried droppings of sea birds used for fertilizer), which Peruvian or Humboldt penguins nest in, has affected

The Hoiho has been badly affected by the destruction of coastal forest. Recent conservation efforts include the building of shelters and tree planting to provide the shy penguin with privacy to nest.

INDEX

First published in 1999 by David Bateman Ltd,
30 Tarndale Grove, Albany Business Park,
Albany, Auckland, New Zealand

First edition for the United States and Canada published
by Barron's Educational Series, Inc., 1999

Text: Judith Hodge, B.A. (Hons)
Photographs: Tui De Roy (The Roving Tortoise) p3 top,
p4 bottom, p10, p18 right; Kim Westerskov (Natural
Images) p6, p8, p16, p20; Key Light Image Library p17;
New Zealand Picture Library all other photographs.
Design: Errol McLeary

All inquiries should be addressed to:
Barron's Educational Series, Inc.
250 Wireless Boulevard
Hauppauge, NY 11788
http://www.barronseduc.com

International Standard Book No. 0-7641-1216-3

Library of Congress Cataloging-in-Publication Data
Walker-Hodge, Judith, 1963–
    Penguins / Judith Hodge.
        p. cm. — (Animals of the oceans)
    Summary: Describes the physical characteristics,
habits, and natural envornment of these flightless
sea birds, which are found only in the southern
hemisphere.
    ISBN 0-7641-1216-3
    1. Penguins—Juvenile literature. [1. Penguins.]
I. Title. II. Series.
QL696.S473W345 1999
598.47—dc21
                                                99-25196
                                                CIP

Printed in Hong Kong
9 8 7 6 5 4 3 2 1